Vagabond Sun

Judita Vaičiūnaitė

Vagabond Sun
—*Selected Poems*—

Translated from Lithuanian
by Rimas Uzgiris

Shearsman Books

First published in the United Kingdom in 2018 by
Shearsman Books
50 Westons Hill Drive
Emersons Green
BRISTOL
BS16 7DF

Shearsman Books Ltd Registered Office
30–31 St. James Place, Mangotsfield, Bristol BS16 9JB
(this address not for correspondence)

www.shearsman.com

ISBN 978-1-84861-620-2

The translator is grateful for an award by the National Endowment for the
Arts, which enabled the great majority of the work on this book to be carried
out, and to the Lithuanian Culture Institute (Lietuvos kultūros institutas)
for an additional grant which enabled its expansion and completion.

Contents

Acknowledgements

AGNI: 'Vilnius. Archaeology'.
Asymptote: 'Old Town (I)', 'Store', 'Blue Earth'.
Bernardinai.lt: 'Girl with Ermine'.
Circumference: 'Three Fates: 1. Nike 2. Red Tunic 3. Witch',
'A Nameless Source'.
The Drunken Boat: 'The Red Dress', 'Pool Hall', 'Vagabond Sun', 'Blossoming
Pear'; from the cycle 'Canon for Barbora Radvilaitė': 5. 'Catherine of the
Habsburgs' 6. 'Sigismund Augustus' 7. 'Barbora Radvilaitė'
Field: 'Extravaganza'.
Gobshite Quarterly: 'Heat', 'Cafés light their fires…', 'Mare's Tails'.
Lituanus: 'VI. My old courtyard' (from the cycle 'To the Only City'),
'Lilacs on Pylimo Street', 'Wagon', 'A Bell from the Vilnius Fair',
'3. Saint Katherine's, or St. Benedictine's' (from the cycle 'Vilnius Churches'),
'Amber Gems', 'Vytis', 'Siauroji Street', 'The Defensive Wall of the City'.
Lumina: 'That Diaphanous Night, 5: …I caress the things you touched:…'
Mayday: 'Every Day', 'Coronation'.
Mid-American Review, Translation Chapbook Series: 'Crystal', 'Four Portraits:
1. Circe, 2. Calypso, 3. Nausicäa, 4. Penelope', from the cycle
'Under Northern Heraldry (1-4, 6-7)'.
Modern Poetry in Translation: 'Street Performer', 'Street Light', 'Ladybug'.
New Humanist: 'The Street Ship'.
Poem Magazine: 'Bend', 'Moonflowers', 'Clear Night', 'A Play',
'Old town apartments burn…'.
Shearsman: 'Anapaestic', 'The yellow-blooming mustard field…',
'I freeze like a pillar of salt…', 'A heart beats below the ice…', 'Air Raid,
'Under Electra's Virginal Statue', 'Concert'.
Vilnius Review: 'Sunday will come…', 'Like Two Beasts of Babylon', 'Feverish
Heat in the City', 'from the cycle Castle, 4: Journey on, merchants and
monks…', 'Sunflower [In Vilnius…]', 'Lullaby', 'By Steamboat',
'Drought (II)', 'To Gather Geraniums Yet', 'I'm Leaving…'.
World Literature Today (Translation Tuesday Blog):
'Fuchsia Branch in the Wind', 'Side-Street Madonna'.

Introduction[1]

Judita Vaičiūnaitė (1937-2001) was a major Lithuanian poet of the second half of the twentieth century. She was born in Kaunas during Lithuania's brief period of independence, a period book-ended by the Russian Empire (from the time of the final, 1795 partition of the Polish-Lithuanian Republic), and the Soviet Union. Her family moved to Vilnius after the Second World War, and she lived the last decade of her life in the newly independent Republic of Lithuania. Her generation produced a number of astonishing poets, among them her friend Tomas Venclova, all of whom, to varying degrees would mark their creative work with resistance to Soviet rule and Soviet ideology. This resistance was often expressed in subtle ways. Closed borders also prevented direct contact with many cultural developments in the west. Thus, although both Lithuania and Great Britain are part of Europe, both part of the "Western" tradition, their cultural spheres diverge enough to call for some commentary. Perhaps of all Western European nations, Ireland is the most similar to Lithuania: small, agrarian, Catholic, possessing a proud pagan past, fated to be the plaything of empires. Yet, they were different empires, with different languages in play. Lithuania, despite the widespread adoption of Polish by the upper classes through the late renaissance up to the modern period, despite the ban on the printed Lithuanian word imposed by czarist Russia in the late 19th century, despite almost a half-century in the Soviet Union, retained its language, and Vaičiūnaitė was one of its masters. It is not an easy language to master. The vocabulary is rich, the nouns have seven declensions, making word order quite free, the verbs have a plethora of possible prefixes giving them nuances unavailable to English without the addition of quite a few words, and Vaičiūnaitė does not give translators much room for addition. Her poetry is compact, precise, the lines short, the line breaks sharp, run-ons (like this and the preceding sentence) are common, and the images come in waves. Not to mention, like most Lithuanian writers, she likes adjectives (the white whale of contemporary English language poetics as taught in MFA programs). As the translator, I have preserved her stylistic features except when the poem was simply not sounding right in English. All translation involves a degree of domestication, and I have tried to keep this degree small. Even in her rhyming poems, I try to make them sing, sometimes

---

[1] Earlier parts of this essay have appeared in the *Vilnius Review, Mid-American Review*, the *AGNI* blog, and *World Literature Today*'s Translation Tuesday blog.

finding the means to preserve her exact rhyme scheme, sometimes merely rhyming some of the lines, or by creating internal rhymes, slant-rhymes, in other words, by trying to signal to the reader the song-like quality of a certain lyric. I do not like to change what a poet is actually saying in terms of thoughts, images, feelings and figurative language. On the other hand, Vaičiūnaitė is a largely unknown poet outside of Lithuania. Few people read Lithuanian. The poems have to "work" as English poems, or they will not be read. And yet they are well worth reading, both for her blending of styles old and new, and for her deeply felt encounter with her city, history, myth, and the general features of human experience. Although she tends to write short, highly compressed poems, when she wants to treat a theme more expansively she writes sequences of such poems. Four complete sequences, or cycles, are included in this selection of her work, organized in general chronological order from her first collection published in 1960, to her last in 2000. In order to further assist the English language reader, I would like to discuss some of the culturally-bound features of her work, helping bring the reader to the author and her poetic world.

One of the cultural differences especially relevant to understanding Vaičiūnaitė's poetry is the relative persistence of neo-romantic strains in Lithuanian literature far into the 20th century, and even into the 21st. Romanticism came late to Lithuanian poetry, the language itself having been banned by the Russian empire after the 1863 uprising. Mairionis, starting in 1895, was the great romantic of Lithuanian literature, articulating Lithuanian identity in relation to nature, Catholicism and ancient history, with a verse of scintillating musicality. Salomėja Neris, the first prominent female poet in Lithuanian, continued this tradition during the mid-twentieth century (with a late twist: she became a diehard communist, even writing an odious encomium to Stalin). A romantic musicality became a hallmark of Lithuanian poetry throughout the 20th century, with themes often drawn from nature and rural life. Although a much longed-for independence from Russia saw the introduction in the twenties of the modernist avant-garde in the work of Kazys Binkis and the Four Winds group, and other modernist influences could be felt in the work of, for example, Henrikas Radauskas, Vincas Mykolaitis-Putinas and Vytautas Mačernis, the full-fledged development of these movements was suppressed after the Soviet annexation of Lithuania in 1940 and its dogmatic imposition of Soviet realist art-values. Annexation went hand in hand with industrialisation and the collectivisation of the agricultural economy. Thus, various means of subtle resistance to Soviet rule became, in literature, a focus on the individual, on subjective experience, on nature and traditional country life, along with references to Lithuania's past. Hence the neo-romanticism. Hence its persistence.[2]

We can see these elements in Vaičiūnaitė's oeuvre as well. Her 'To Gather Geraniums Yet' uses rhyming quatrains in a paean to flowers. The narrator, sunk in wintry gloom, in a lonely city flat, darning her ripped tights – a sign of the general Soviet poverty – draws strength and hope from the natural world's manifestation of beauty and renewal:

> each day deeper yet – January,
> into the jaws of solitude's flat,
> to carry the profile secretly,
> like the germ of life, by the heart.

Like a number of her poems, "To Gather Geraniums Yet" intertwines the modernist alienation of a city dweller with the neo-romantic valorization of nature. The natural world provides the source of inspiration, meaningful connection, life itself. The drudgery of daily life, urban dirt and grit, is placed in negative contrast to the blooming flowers. Vaičiūnaitė positions herself as part of the Lithuanian neo-romantic tradition stylistically as well, composing the poem in rhyming quatrains. Urban existence was largely a new phenomenon for the previously (mostly) agrarian Lithuanian culture, and this poem exemplifies Vaičiūnaitė's effort to give this new form of life expression, even if, at this stage it is seen in a negative light.

The traditional, formal style evident in 'To Gather Geraniums Yet' was only one of her modes. Vaičiūnaitė came to adapt her poetics to urban existence, breaking apart her lines in stanzas, building run-on sentences on top of each other, connecting (or disconnecting) phrases with dashes, using ellipses to create pauses and gaps...

> Cupolas, columns, bridges floating by,
> time will swim beyond the window,
> and we'll forget that it's even there...

---

[2] One could argue that similar features were present in the field of Lithuanian painting where expressionism was a dominant mode through the end of the 20th century. The Danish artist Henrik Anderson, who has been coming to teach at the Vilnius Art Academy for years, has said, in conversation, that he was amazed that art was consistently and exclusively understood until very recently from the perspective of the subject, in terms of personal expression.

Sunday will come.
And seven lamps will smash into flour.
Dawn will break as coloured confetti.
      (*from* 'Sunday will come…')

The changes in style go hand in hand with a more nuanced thematic treatment of urban life. The city, dirty as it is, prone to leaving the individual alienated, also comes to be seen as a source of possibility, pleasure, a meeting ground and a locus of history.

I live by day –

      wild, lonely, choking
      with joy.
On dusty, burnt-out cobblestones,
      we jump –
      into a deceiving light
            (*from* 'Feverish heat in the city…')

Stylistically, these innovations were revolutionary for the Lithuanian lyric, helping drag it out of a traditional, romantic past into the modern world. In this act, she was not alone, but one of a generation of late 20th century poets who were part of what can be called a second modernist revolution in Lithuanian literature. Together with Tomas Venclova, Sigitas Geda, Marcelijus Martinaitis, and Vytautas Bložė, she pushed lyrical language and its forms of expression in new directions. What marks her work, besides her stylistic innovations, as especially different from so many others was its incorporation of the city's layout and architecture, urban life, and the city's historical roots (Tomas Venclova was closest to her in this endeavour). In the poem, 'Vilnius. Archaeology', she digs down, uncovers the past, searching for that identity, the source of who we are. Vilnius is Lithuanian because of its distant past (which is not Polish, not Russian, not Soviet), and her poems uncover this heritage. 'Vilnius. Archaeology' also represents this new stylistic development in Vaičiūnaitė's poetic form: fractured, meandering lines linked by dashes and commas, with sharp and sudden contrasts, juxtapositions and enjambments. We might even speculate that her attention to the city, and to the old town of Vilnius in particular, led her to this form of fractured unity. Urbanites, one might say, are both connected and apart. The Baroque streets wind this way and that, yielding unexpected vistas, surprising twists and turns.

Formally, she enacts the city. Tender lyricism is cut with violence and foreboding. History has been unkind, after all. Randomness, sudden change, and danger are parts of her city life as much as the beautiful facade, the church bells, and the cobbled streets. She is both meditative and imagistic. Clear and mysterious. Her observations – compressed, linked together often in a cascade of phrases connected by commas and dashes – might even lead us to see her as a kind of Dickinson from the other end of the Western tradition. She breaks apart traditional lyrical structures without ever losing a finely tuned sense of sound. Her work took the old romantic themes and styles, moved them into the city and made them modern. It was an achievement whose rootedness may turn out to be universal.

We cannot fail to mention how, in this late 20th century context, in a poetic culture dominated by men (the reader may have noticed that the poet's generational peers listed above were all male), she gave voice to women's experiences, especially to love, sexuality and being a single mother. The poem 'Lullaby', dedicated to her daughter, connects Lithuanian folklore, the grubbiness of the city, and her own relationship to her child: "and a slender voice sounds from the gutter's slop: / – Rock-a-bye baby, my forgotten one – – // That voice from fairytales lulls like a rustling..." Here, as in 'To Gather Geraniums Yet', the sheer grit of the urban experience undercuts neo-romanticism's temptation to senti-mentalise nature and the past by treating the urban as an inescapable part of our existence. We cannot simply escape to the sunny fields and live in some Arcadian fantasy. When a lullaby comes out of "the gutter's slop", or flowers break through pavement cracks, and weeds bloom among Old Town ruins, neither nature's beauty, nor the past, are unproblematically given. One has to look hard through the dust to see what is really there, and what is there turns out to be a complex interwoven tapestry of concrete, steel, nature, folklore, history and people of all kinds.

Vaičiūnaitė's poems also, importantly, give us an interior, lyrical experience of female desire. With few exceptions, Salomėja Nėris before her, Janina Degutytė and Nijolė Miljauskaitė overlapping with her, the Lithuanian poetic world was masculine. Love poetry was the love of women, but with Vaičiūnaitė we finally see the other – equivalently powerful – side of the coin, the poetry of a women loving men, of a single mother no less. Not surprisingly, her love poetry intersects with work that expresses the struggle against the restraints of a patriarchal world. Iconic imagistic poems like 'The Red Dress' take the liberation of female sexuality as a necessity, if not an anticipated fact about the future. Is "Coronation" a poem about an unrecognised woman in patriarchal society crowning herself with quotidian regalia? Is it also a political poem, written as it was during the Soviet era, in which the "drunken king of clubs" is a Soviet Premier? Vaičiūnaitė often lets her images do their work, leaving open various interpretive possibilities.

Another unique feature of Vaičiūnaitė's work is the use of the dramatic monologue applied to historical and mythological characters, who were often also women. In this, we can see some overlap with Constantine Cavafy, at least in terms of the treatment of modern love in the city and the dramatic historical monologue in language that is both modernist and traditional in style and voice. Both her monologues and her city poems are often concerned with history. As is consistent with her oeuvre, history and mythology are usually, and unusually for her time and place, addressed from a female perspective. These themes can even intertwine with modern city life, as when urban women in high heels become Barboras: the 17th century beauty who entranced a king against the opposition of his mother (the Machiavellian Bona Sforza), and who died suddenly, mysteriously within a year of her marriage. Vaičiūnaitė often speaks directly from the perspective of these historical and mythological characters, not unlike Cavafy. We can see this most effectively in her cycle of poems, 'Canon for Barbora Radvilaite', which treats the above-mentioned historical love story through seven monologues, each spoken by a historical figure (or two, in the case of the brothers), though one is an unnamed artisan (perhaps a stand-in for the poet?). The historical story and its characters have, in Lithuanian discourse, taken on the quality of myth, becoming a defining moment for Lithuanians (though, ironically perhaps, since none of the aristocratic personages would have been speaking Lithuanian). One could argue that it is not just a love story in which a Polish-speaking Vilnius family features prominently in the history of the Polish crown, but that Barbora's story encapsulates a feeling of Lithuania betrayed by the Polish, by the political machinations that left the Lithuanian part of the union in perennial second place, weakened and unsupported before being swallowed up by the Russian Empire. Then again, it's also simply a compelling love story enmeshed within Europe's multicultural aristocratic interrelations.

Vaičiūnaitė delves into Greek mythology as well, giving voice to women at the margins of classical stories. She uses these characters to bring to fore perspectives that have been left out of the literary and historical imagination of Lithuania, if not the world. An example of this would be her cycle, 'Four Portraits', in which four women from Homer's *Odyssey* are given extensive monologues in which they express their love for Odysseus and their dismay at his leaving them. They are tender poems that seem to capture the first moments of shock as the loved one prepares to leave, like snapshots of the first consciousness of abandonment.

Another way in which Vaičiūnaitė transcends her cultural bounds is how her poems can work to expand cultural identity beyond narrow nationalistic frameworks. Here, the city poems are fundamental again. Vilnius has a complex past, having been part of many countries and home to many ethnicities. Vaičiūnaitė strays from the standard neo-romantic nationalist mode by incorporating this diverse history into her work. She can claim Vilnius for Lithuanians, while also leaving space for others. Thus, we can see how the poem from the cycle 'Castle' deepens and broadens Lithuanian identity by connecting it to Vilnius' unique, multicultural history. Its Whitmanesque long lines break under the weight of the experiences packed into them. Vilnius, her 'Babylon', is broken, packed with "so many tongues" (Babel?). It needs to be rebuilt, not on narrow nationalist models (i.e. "blood and soil"), but in a way that reflects its variegated and welcoming past.

> Silversmiths, salt-sellers and cobblers,
> > may you live here in concord.
> All homeless wanderers of goodwill –
> > may you build this Vilnius.

As we saw with 'To Gather Geraniums Yet', Vaičiūnaitė by no means ignores the neo-romantic emphasis on nature, but does something different by bringing it into the city, integrating those traditional values with her actual lived urban experience, layered as it is with different cultures over its long history. 'Sunflower' expands on the earlier poem by granting more sustained attention to the specific interaction of nature, city and history, with less focus on the subject's experiences, and with the broken lines characteristic of her urban poetics.

> a flower of green, alien blood,
> > as if sprouting from the Vilnius baroque,
> it rocked its noble head up high
> > above the sleepy heat of scattered

bricks, above debris,
above foundations previously unseen,
above the medieval town

As in the case of Vaičiūnaitė and Cavafy, here too we can point to co-evolutionary phases in her Eastern European poetics with (the rest of) the West. 'Sunflower' calls to mind Allen Ginsberg's 'Sunflower Sutra' in its evocation of the lone city flower growing through debris, gazing through dust, the dust of the city, and the dust of history. It's "alien" blood exemplifies otherness. In the original, Vaičiūnaitė wrote "Indian" (i.e. Native American). I generalised the translation to bring to the fore the sense in which almost all the inhabitants of post-war Vilnius were "aliens", that is, they came from elsewhere to inhabit a city largely emptied (through murder or relocation) of its Polish and Jewish inhabitants. Indeed, the lost presence of the once vibrant Jewish population is alluded to in her haunting 'Lilacs on Pylimo Street'. Vaičiūnaitė herself was born in Kaunas (the interwar capital, Vilnius having been illegally and forcibly annexed by Poland in 1920). Her family moved to Vilnius after the war. Most other leading poets of Lithuania were from town and country (with the exception of Venclova). Vaičiūnaitė's urban, multicultural perspective is rooted in her personal history, which is also one of dislocation, of being "other" in one's home (Vilnius). Notice how in 'Sunflower', she positions the flower on Tartar Street, named after the Central Asian peoples who both fought against and for Lithuania in the years of the Grand Duchy, some of whom remain as a minority culture. Layers of history intertwine: "the medieval town", "the Vilnius baroque", "the royal summer park", "the iron stubble". We are all alien, and yet we can all belong, drawing on our shared nature. We just need to see through the dust.

Rimas Uzgiris, Ph.D., MFA
Vilnius University

Vagabond Sun

Every Day

When words are ripped from the husk of the room,
and shredded papers scatter like shards,
I hear, every day – in the nexus of streets,
by the mouth of the river – your living pulse.
       You – a diving suit.
You – a city of shrieking glass, cliffs and concrete.
It takes strength to emerge from these four walls
so that my strophes, poured from sun, thunder and nerves,
might, like bowls, collect the yellow summer sky…

* * *

The yellow-blooming mustard field.
     Oneness and sun.
A mood –
     like the turning of a hurdy-gurdy.
Edges grow dull,
     and in the warm, round world
something else,
     clear and weighty,
     climbs my throat.
Bitter yellow distances…
     I'm waiting for a miracle,
vainly trying to forget
     yesterday and myself.
All that's left is the rolling mustard sun –
     a state of weightlessness –
and love, gifting me the meaning
     of tears and wind…

Don't Be Afraid

– for V. R.

If you think of me as a ray,
      I will be that for you –
and shine at midnight on delicate grass…
Let the most beautiful summer be ours –
never to burden your shoulders with reproof.
And if clouds creep up and pour
their cold, slick rain on summer's heart,
don't be afraid.
      I'm a ray – golden, warm…
Broken in a tear
      to shine more brightly than before.

from the cycle To the Only City

VI

My old courtyard is also a part of Vilnius:
its spacious square, its thick stone walls,
the clothes hung out to dry, all noise and light,
the wind spills over the fence all day and night…

The hollow echo of dusty streets is hardly heard…
Windows, windows all around… Shining eyes of glass.
Grey pigeons wade through the day in melting snow
with blushing feet… They come and go…

How many people have passed through these gates!
What variety of footsteps fend the courtyard's ways!
Perhaps those others gazed upon it all the same –
these glimmering roofs, these fluttering wings…

Maybe their smiles and tears have now seeped
into my old courtyard – this little piece of Vilnius…
Maybe for that reason the walls glow with sunlight,
trying to tell us something, full of lucid life…

Side-Street Madonna

Wistful and empty. Skies squirt rain.
Pipes rust along an old stone wall…
Does my saint still stand flush
in the bell-tower niche? Ave Maria.

Maybe I'll meet her – hatless, wet,
shivering on the sidewalk, silent…
Above the pot-holed, cobblestoned streets
dusk lies heavy, dusk swims on.

I love that small, side-street Madonna –
her paint peeling, her feet missing…
I accept her smile like a loaf of bread
and divide it up for a thousand lips.

Her face is familiar, her face quotidian –
they drove a girl into the street today…
A shadow quivers on bell-tower walls:
the niche crumbles, falls… Ave Maria.

For the Unknown Cabiria

Under the bridge – a unique life. The colours and lights of the dregs.
A unique echo – when the iron above resounds with footsteps and wheels,
when the water's black lengthens the yellow luminescence of lamplights.
The world of the damned.
The world of those forgotten.
In the water's black, drowned roofs and bell towers are overturned,
the charred river blooms with red and green advertisements –
the smoke of illusions.
Under the bridge, you can dream of authentic eternal light
when your dress, buoyant like a rainbow in the wind,
flutters above the railings…
Under the bridge, you can dream that he will come and understand,
forgiving all – so that you fly across the bridge's black as if to light…
Cigarette butts and spit, the night's profanities, stifling laments
melt into the water's black…
Death, sin, and sorrow – in the water's black…
Maunder under the bridge. You'll carry it:
the blackest terror, the oppressive drone – you'll lift the bridge
onto your fragile shoulders…

from the cycle That Diaphanous Night

5.

...I caress the things you touched:
a doorknob, an old tablecloth –
　　　they seem so beautiful to me.
Hot coffee steams...
　　　And the evening begins to spill
into the window that ices like smoke
　　　until it casts the stained-glass of stars.
Lustreless, violet snowflakes fall
　　　like soft stains, and trolleybuses
murmur in the dark. The wind moans through the square...
Nobody waits for me in the empty, quaint café,
but I smile all evening long,
　　　warmly, plainly – like a child...
I wait all evening long...
　　　The chessboard floor melts
into greenish mist as the mirror is covered in smoke.
A second – an instant – comes back to life – in marvellous darkness...
...I love those walls most where your breath just came to its end.

* * *

Sunday will come.
      We will cover our bread with kisses and butter.
We will scan, haphazardly, the circus posters
and wander
      through the motley, noisy city of sun
like two naughty children.

When midday sticks like dust between the teeth,
we'll fill our mugs with tawny beer,
and surrounded by bar smoke –
      packed in the cabin of that boat,
we will not dare to cuddle with our brothers.

Cupolas, columns, bridges floating by,
time will swim beyond the window,
      and we'll forget that it's even there…
Sunday will come.
      And seven lamps will smash into grain.
Dawn will break as coloured confetti.

* * *

I'm leaving.
     My dress opens like an old parachute:
I never owned
     so much wind, so much space…
Neighbourhoods rotate below me
     like a postcard stand,
and an ancient pear tree
     burns white as a dandelion by the gate.
Like a soap bubble
     I expand in multi-coloured suns,
bribing the streets
     with my hoarse hum, barely heard…
So I drink a handful of water
     from a rusty fountain,
and, except for the dawning of warm days,
     take nothing with me for the road…

from the cycle Room on the Dunes

1. Inlet

We're feeding the gulls at the inlet.
      The wind blows through my sodden raincoat.
My weathervane – a motley shawl. The soapy sea
      pales with northern sky.
I'm bringing you a seagull's uncertain feeling
      that answers to the protean sea
where birds squack rapaciously,
      cold sand squeaks, and schooners don't return.
But the film goes on. The birds perch on my shoulders.
      Delayed in their dark cries, I feel
bright trains stopping behind our backs
      in the asphalt town.
And foreign, shabby furniture shivers
      in the room on the dunes – amazed
that I'm smiling, hiding my eyes
      in the hot, dry palms of your hands.

Juodkrantė

Here it smells of Curonian sweat, heat, and pines.
Here the wind writes its chronicles on sand…
　　　　How can I know you,
little amber god,
　　　　brought here by sand and steel,
by the babel of dead words
　　　　melting in the wind, forgotten?…

Only the sun as then, when forests became amber,
turns like the first mother's primordial millstones.

Four Portraits

1. Circe

… and time ran unheeded…

Forgive me – they are only a drove of pigs.
     I herd them from trough to pen.
But if you're feeling sad,
     they can sit as extras around the rotating banquet table…
And the ancient song of goblets, and the flickering torches,
     will beat out their hexameter verse,
and the eyes of my ancient statue
     will come to life with a mocking gleam…
Then, fires gone out, the tripod will fall mute.
     Enchantments will wane.
     My own hands will toss away the poisoned pot.
And Circe will submit to the marvellous one…
     While you… You will go like a madman
     into the calling light to feast.
I will not keep you by force.
     So sail – if you are afraid to anger fate,
     to cut the red thread of the plot…
Here are skeins of wine for the journey.
     I offer my wisdom, my tenderness.
This raft of splintered logs will carry you
     to the unmapped cliffs of an Ithaca that never was.
O that you would not see
     how proud eyes shine wide with sorrow,
I separate from you unseen.
     I was generous. And kept my word.
Strange man, to have forsaken me.
     My only…
     I love you, Odysseus.

2. Calypso

...he didn't love the pretty nymph, despite resting in her bright chamber,
in her bed...

Not with the brightness of their cheeks,
>nor with the luxuriance of their hair,
>nor in height did any equal me...
But the gods are jealous of my happiness.
>I fear their wrath. I am building a boat.
>I bring you axe and auger.
I stitched your sails myself –
>those wings, tearing up time,
>that flag, swift and straight,
and you want me in the blink of an eye,
>and you withdraw, only to caress
>my elegant waist again.
I am jealous beyond measure, jealous of them all:
>your wife and your dogs,
>your distant, foreign land...
This role is too difficult to play.
>Why give a goddess this passion, vexing and painful,
>as if to some little, flour-covered miller's girl?
For seven years,
>I tied you with my hands, my hair, my caresses...
>Humiliated,
I still want for you too
>to be immortal like the stars in the sky...
>But you spilled the ambrosia,
and having fled from a loving embrace,
>you mourned, burying your face in the sand –
>yet I left no regret in your heart...
In the overgrown, flowering grotto, only the sea understands me.
>I wanted what was good for you.
>I love you, Odysseus.

3. Nausicaä

Safe journeys, wanderer, and when you return to your homeland, see that you don't forget me...

I have not yet kissed a man.
    And my voice is like a wave.
    And my body doesn't know the touch of manly hands.
But I longed for one such as you.
    We were both intoxicated
    by fatigue and wonder.
Blessed and cursed will be that ball
    which we tossed upon the shore,
    the washing hung to dry,
and two ridiculous mules,
    in that golden, antique morning,
    pulling my little cart...
I – Nausicaä, am of seafaring stock.
    And I own something
    from that boat of happiness I met dying on the shore.
And joy – this purple wool
    spun by my mother. And my father's
    open home – high and hospitable.
So under an ancient sky, we toast, royally,
    simply, the unexpected guest.
Why do you hide tears under your hood –
    we are not trying to question you:
    strong, unfathomable and free...
Pressed to a column, I melt into it...
    Let there be silence –
    I stood as if alone in the great hall
because no one will ever know
    what I felt at that time –
what I refuse to admit even to myself:
    I love you, Odysseus.

4. Penelope

...I would go to the grave with the name Odysseus in my heart...

It's hard for one who has experienced your love –
    nobody can replace you,
    nobody is worthy of you.
And why am I to blame
    that I wait for you for years,
    going deaf while all in the great hall whistle and clap.
And why am I to blame
    that the town, the suitors and slaves all laugh.
And why am I to blame
    that I remain the boring and eccentric Penelope.
I want the hearth to shine for you
    through the husk of these walls, through time.
    Pure, like an idea,
I want to save some limpid water for you, untouched,
    in a brimming amphora.
Let all the generations of women
    feel the waiting that fills my heart
whenever they hear the sea sighing in a shell
    or gaze into an empty room.
Yet I am one of those to whom one returns.
    The faithful kind.
    Famous evermore for patience and wisdom.
I will wipe away the blood from your hands
    using my very own hair, my lips.
I will cry by your knees out of joy.
    I love you, Odysseus.

* * *

Cafés light their fires…
    With smoke, rain, cocktails,
an out of tune piano – lines
    that smell of asters.
With wet, wan clothes,
    covered by a black shawl,
I walk alone into the unreal, ephemeral reel.
Somewhere in the foothills of giant buildings,
searchlights cut my body out of the muddle of cars…
    One heals
from love, from autumn…
    Lights colour the pallid face
while darkness covers the tables –
    a false film.

Lullaby

– for Ula

Summer on the banks. Laundering by night in the river…
Moonlight cools the balcony's tin.
Wires from street lights sway like bridges
and a slender voice sounds from the gutter's slop:
– Rock-a-bye baby, my forgotten one –

That voice from fairytales lulls like a rustling…
Somewhere in the subconscious – rushes in the mist,
the harsh light of the moon (I was born on a Monday)…
To the rhythm of a nighttime intersection, I rock my firstborn:
– Rock-a-bye baby, my forgotten one –

Under Northern Heraldry

1. The Gates of the City

Dawn. Chimneys and bell-towers sharpen.
    The gates of the city shine.
Arrow slits close up.
    Shadows, and the sounds of battle, fade.
In vain would you be the fog and rain –
    you who unfold to the northern sun…
In the wild glow of fires,
    as chapel candles and constellations drip,
above the hills,
    above the rise and fall of roofs,
    the bells peal,
so much space, such flight…
    Cracked pavement obeys the rule of time.
I kiss your bricks,
    your coat of arms,
    your rippling, gentle name,
and raise my rusty keys…
    Dawn. The gates of the city shine.

2. Bridge Street

The noise of markets and booths fades
      with the sighs of guards and customs-men.
Like ripples in a river, the pale voices
      of unknown urbanites
      melt into forgetfulness...
But the city's river will still flow
      in a stream that is limpid,
      turgid, and original.
In a lane that could be a highway, stone turns white
      under fog, ashes and dust...
The pole stars of the streets are strong and deep.
      Angular roofs slip
      into the current of time,
past the indelible glimmer of water,
      crumbling buttresses,
      rainbows in the gateways,
and old fences like hand rails...
      Yet, we will splatter the cobblestones
      with the light of spring,
and let the twentieth century ring with the tapping heels
      of Barboras gazing out from under black shawls.

3. Shadows

ICI
REPOSE
MAXIMILIEN
TRUZZI
(Directeur de cirque)
Né à Guardia Ferrarese
(Italia) 1833
Decedé le 16 avril 1899
– Rasų Cemetery

From the jester's dancing fingers rise

dark droll shadows –

shadows

that climb crosses, sculptures and wet chapel marble.

The flux of them

stipples the crumbling, cemetery wall.

Poplars stretch like cries –

wild, long and mad.

Under northern greyness, under the wings of crows,

a forgotten circus plays.

And a rusty, horse's head neighs on a flippant grave.

The rain is full

of the orange-coloured scent of orange rinds.

Masks will crumble,

and what is real is clay – your appointed place on the globe

– – – – – – – – – – – – – – – – – pray for us, or applaud.

4. Seagulls

Through tightly serried houses,
      seagulls penetrate lanes
to tussle among street lamps,
      between tight, lighted lofts
and cinematic Old Town roofs,
      municipal buildings, weathervanes –
and smoke, lying like a sheet on the cobblestones,
      cannot cover them up
because the call remains –
      because it is everywhere (what ears cannot contain),
because the wind threads their voice from afar – long and slender,
because they are uncountable
      on balconies, bridges, and arcades,
and on the crosses of campaniles,
      and on scaffolds and stairs…

5. The Market of Used Goods

Icons. Books. Mirrors.

                        Children's shoes.

                                     Crematorium

heat blaring from the sun.

                         pick one

Feel the press. A baby with dirty wool socks. Heat.

A drunken gypsy. Old women under faded, flowered umbrellas.

He was so handsome

                those blue

                     forget it

                         madam

Forget it. The attraction of antiques. Fashions of another day.

The scent of your childhood flat.

                               A voice from the grave, woven into noise.

Fragile like a stranger's shabby bed-clothes –

                              brotherhood.

6. Antiquarians

A brick wall ices over.
      Yellow, archival chrysanthemums
freeze on the glass.
      Streets are etchings.
      Night – from old books.
Only my face is warm from kisses…
      Snow and more snow in the dark
lashes the heraldry above the store,
      and time denies that I will lose you.
Only the white tower will turn black, sometime –
      in the last week of March.
Only the river will froth under ice, under arches
      of narrow, rusty bridges…

A silent film, projected onto bricks,
      has concluded, somehow, on its own
that the shining, wet face, like a street lamp,
      will not melt in the morning.

7. Courtyard with Arcades

Spring will come again,
      and snow will slip away
      like the sound of a harpsichord,
dirty, courtyard galleries
      will be filled with a blue
      and unctuous fog
that stains the linens left out to dry…
      That one evening.
      That one time.
Then it fades – like ink stains
      left on abandoned tables –
      like the Renaissance…
Then, once more, these northern arches
      will be covered with fragile ice,
      the same again, yet different.
And in a darkened, Italianate yard
      like a small and empty auditorium,
passing by the gates you'll hear
      the sound of those long gone –
      watchmen and horses…
Someone will take tea…
      Tracing in the twilight of arcades
      the persistence of symmetry and sun…

* * *

Feverish heat in the city:
     you serve me mother's wine
     with the dog rose's red sun.
We form an arch at night –
     grown together in our embrace.
I live by day –
     wild, lonely, choking
     with joy.
On dusty, burnt-out cobblestones,
     we jump –
     into a deceiving light
full of childish want, worry, and woe.
Mulled wine stains
     my dress, the floor, the earth.
Arches of clasping hands.
     The dog rose burns.
     June.

* * *

Mare's tails.
Mad sun. Mare's tails on the precipice.
The shriek
of steamboats on the river –
receding, half-empty.
Mare's tails.
Green swings falling at breakneck speeds.
Mare's tails. Lust. A heretical height
offered by you.
Mare's tails.

A Play

Can we begin?
      First, the curtain's ghostly flight.
Old programs speckled with signatures.
      Someone is singing in the rain.
The black feathers of fans are rustling
      while sad, decrepit hats droop.
My black-gloved hand begins to quiver
      with feelings I cannot know…

The old flask scent of November –
      dripping from chandeliers
(searchlights shine at night
      on Moniuszko's monument;
      while wind keens
for the dead, for the dirt, cars drone).
      Yet I will forget everything
just so you would not be sad,
      my drunken prompter – gone astray.

I bend down in the middle of a darkened square –
      rotting leaves
fly to me –
      applause resounds
      in an empty house.

The Red Dress

A red dress throbs on a rope
     like a torch left behind.
Moaning, clawing pines
     assault the hotel window.
Someone washed the dress at dawn.
     Someone wrung it out.
     Endless,
the radiance. The weather –
     mindlessly sunny, humid, and sharp.
A red dress throbs on a rope –
     yet still, it will break free.

Pool Hall

The green flatlands crack and split.
      Go. Slice the pool-hall silence
with the solitary steps of a child
      (in the gathering shadows of men),
through the grass of horse-tracks, pitches and pastures
      (the shadows are now six),
through the flattened field for airplanes –
      shadowy, luxuriant, wet –
into the deepening dark (it will soon explode)
      hurry (let no one block out
the light of your eyes)…
      But greenery is more bitter each day
in the world full of shadows and heat
      (a distant white crash –
the sun rolls over an empty green plain
      to meet with catastrophe…).

* * *

Old Town apartments burn with tile stoves.
The window opens – the universe.
      Red bullfinches warble.
Your square, covered in snow, fills with sky.
      Your poems are coal black, smoky –
fire sparks in their layers.
You gave me white wine that will not freeze.
      You gave me the dark radiance of poetry.

Through the blizzard I carry
a baroque bundle
      of city, simile, and love.
(While Atlases shoulder a beaten balcony on my way.)

Three Fates

1. Nike

Lemon rinds,
      the taste of cinnamon,
      wine from the Balkans, drunk.
O morning – so clean,
      belonging not to God,
      nor people, nor the devil,
in such an empty apartment,
      in heated tin and glare of glass,
in a white
circle –
      in the madness of June's sun –
      I lie like a cross, and tears are for naught.
For these broken, battered wings –
      dust shining above the street –
for my naked, wincing shoulders in the light,
      I hate you –
      but open my mouth
to your ghastly purple gale…

2. Red Tunic

A woman with a red tunic
      in the plazas of the world,
a woman at a microphone –
      anguish augments her voice,
wandering among the landless crowds,
      pale and petite,
splashed by a breaking wave,
      stormy, salty and bright…
She sings.
      Ears stuffed with wax
      – the night's black un-ravelers
can't hear.
      Greece – a vast concentration camp.
      You had to leave,
tying yourself to the mast…
      The weapons of the vanquished rust:
stacks of shields, spears and helms.
      The Sirens' hands – bound and bloodstained.

3. Witch

The midday square – stifling and loud.
      (Movie theatres – empty.)
They swarm. And a fierce, subhuman curiosity
      unites thousands.
A pillar of shame grows above houses
      like a strange, desiccated tree.
And my gaze is full of pride –
      delirious and dying.
(The typhus wards, saunas, gulag
      barbers are packed.
Cut hair lies in red bands.)
      And anger flows –
incomprehensible,
      as if I were born on a different planet.
And raving voices throb –
      hoarse from dull pleasure.
A heavy chain chafes my neck.
      The hangman grows bored.
(He tosses empty bottles under the table
      with a mad crash.)
Truth – from my childish mouth,
      wild, untouched.
Light it. My body longs
      for a cleansing flame.

* * *

I freeze like a pillar of salt,
stunned,
in front of my crumbling Old Town –
where a house burns
overgrown with frozen vines:
calligraphic characters under icy windows
crack off eaves and fall...

A hot, fetid backdraught
cuts through the sidestreet.
It accompanies a company of soldiers
headed to the sauna, a red light wavering in the leader's hand.
The smell of sweat returns. I gather voices and shadows,
forced to thaw out.

Heat

Burn yellow, sky…
     As I run in the elemental sun of the sea.
Sparkle, salt…
     My lips chafe from heat.
I call you with wild, naked arms
     wound by juniper thongs,
with wrists of bronze –
     I surrender to the white and wayward sand.
Take me. I surrender – to the bliss
     of your grim liberty,
clean as dunes and drought,
     rustling with the strident shadows
of dog rose, honeysuckle and spruce,
     until the axe
cuts to my heart…
     I am
     because you water me.

Canon for Barbora Radvilaitė

1. Elisabeth of the Habsburgs

I begin.
      Scarcely more than a child, marble-white,
pure, they say, a rare beauty. I married
into a dreary foreign land, ravaged by plague,
where no faithful page kept watch, where frozen

shoulders shivered, shaken with sickness. Yet,
I melted in Sigismund's palms like a ball of snow.
Homesick for wet-nurse, sisters, friends, I was fated
to fall in the piercing fog of a cold and alien city…

Don't trouble me now, you all.
      I never got in your way, Barbora.
When trees sprang into bloom, I died like a nun,
watching the happy couple recede from sight.
My train of fog was carried away by kids.

2. Queen Bona

Both of the brides are dead.
      No one can now prove
if I gave them poison in Venetian glass…
Death is full of irony: I myself was poisoned.
Give me my lute. I'm bored. I'll play.

Without wanting to, I became the hand of fate,
      an old theatre mask.
Blood always dries by the Sforza name.
Everything was done, madly, painfully for my son.
But now in ballroom mirrors – I'm alone, as once…

Maybe the wives died on their own.
      Maybe there is no need to curse
that woman who flaunted the curse to love.
But be on your guard, Barbora – a barbarian,
even sick. I hate you for your love,
      and decree your destiny: death.

3. Mikolojus Radvila "the Red",
Mikolojus Radvila "the Black"

We turned you into the queen of chess and cards.
On a velvet pillow, we brought you a crown
that never touched proud Radvila head before –
for you it became a bleeding bush of thorns.

We pushed and pulled you in various deals –
        first, for the sake of old Goštautas,
a pile of ashes. Then we incarcerated love
in sceptre and coffin.
        We wanted your beauty
to choke death itself –
        a curse on those who slandered us.

We crossed swords on thresholds –
        turned the king's passion
and power into our family's highest regard.
The king's loved ones died nameless.
        We made you, sending letters
from the window, eternal on our coat of arms.

4. Unknown Artist

Eyes brimming charm, brimming sadness, embodied
in this old frame, I painted you –
      Madonna of the north.
I remember how you cried for your dead baby
and then suddenly smiled. You waited only

for Sigismund's words. Your face marked
by long and fateful suffering... I would take you
out of the halls, and into the yard. I painted you
with no crown or halo: just a poor, commoner's cowl.
      In a few hundred years,

Vilnius jewellers will cover you in luxurious clothes,
decorated with gold rose, tulip, and acanthus leaves,
They will raise you into the chapel above the city's gates. Now,
finally, the sky is yours, blinding everyone with its dawn...

5. Catherine of the Habsburgs

Because of you – I was left faceless.
     My features are smoke.
I lie in the far hearth of history, all but ashes.
Sigismund mourned you, pushing me aside,
disgusted to the point of pain…
     But let us not disseminate harms.

I was small when my sister married Sigismund.
I laughed through the engagement, biting the hard apple.
I saw how our crazy grandmother made the sign
of the cross every morning over the hoffräuleins.
     I pressed on,

yet it was not my sister's soul that stood between us – but you.
Like a sword in bed –
     Barbora's name separated us.
I returned to my homeland. After questioning,
they laughed at me.
     I remain silent as a rusted bell.

6. Sigismund Augustus

I sat like a dog at your side as you lay dying
those many months when neither charm, nor beauty
remained – only spirit, only sorrow – as all others
shunned you – you for whom bells used to ring…

You remain for me the same courtly dreamer –
red and hot, giving light. And I am afraid, again,
to get close. Burned by the saltiness of tears,
by the coolness of your hair, which no portrait captures….
        Really –

Will I lose you? Will you disappear? What is a king's realm
if we are stuck in this wasteland – two alone in the world?
Nothing else matters to me – your saintly hours still pulse,
and your gentle fingers have not grown cold in my hands…

7. Barbora Radvilaitė

Like parchment that doesn't yellow, I will not age.
Love will be my power of endurance, like lines for the poet.
I was born here.
      I became the renaissance of Vilnius.
From here I take my charm, the allure this place maintains.

Once dead, I returned. My coffin was dark and tight.
Beyond it – the rhythm of hoofs like the ticking of a clock.
Beyond it – the sighs of Sigismund, hollow and hot.
Once dead, I returned – believing in my own sky.

To this city in a fog – to the damp, humid glow
of its towers, to the warm, salving rain
I came.
      They didn't force coronation, but once exiled,
they brought me back.
      And I rose again – having touched this ground.

* * *

A heart beats below the ice –
      Prussian, Livonian, Etruscan.
My pillow is wet with tears –
      come back, like the continuous cloud
of dust that follows marching armies,
      and look, with salty sea glare
into my heart,
      and speak – maybe
the pallid forms will move on a shield,
      or on a broken vase…
      Because no one
ever dies – we are only oppressed
      by the filthy snow of thaws.

Extravaganza

There is a woman in a black musketeer's hat
among the violet houses and strange courtyards
overgrown with moss – children and vagabonds
shout until hoarse. Heavy as a sailor's chest,

the gate will open, and I'll walk, tentatively,
through the bluish glass of broken bottles.
Cobwebs – the decay of sails, we are in
the time of old records. (With a kiss,

I'll mark you.) The dusty, rickety banisters
cannot hold our dreams. Stick close to the walls.
The sweet song of a yellow wind, grasses –
the bird store – parrots, canaries, hummingbirds…

Vagabond Sun

Despite her light hair, you know
      she's a gypsy.
Through the hum of the faucet, in the cemented night,
a saxophone heats up the dark (don't come here
to berate street urchins, the heat, or the begging dog).
      And the skirt –
flowered like a field (how perfectly lacking in taste!)
stuns the proper world. It is, after all, borrowed
from taverns, train stations and fairs…

      It's not clear what is missing,
but words will spread
      like the hearts of faded cards,
and we should open our veins in the dusty market-place
(the blood gushes as suddenly
      as summer rain),
until again, in humid chambers,
      alarm clocks begin to sing,
and you'll see that dawn is boundless,
      the sun – a vagabond.

Blossoming Pear

But an old armchair in the corner by the door,
washed now by such muddy rain,
but the rooms full of mist and smoke,
steeped in the pale, sleepy sun,
but your time is melted into mine,
a happy, sad time, while the pear tree blooms
looking pitifully thin in the mirror –
unreal as lace…
                Probably
the blossoms will fall, but I will love you,
and blank walls will shine like mother-of-pearl…

Only the smell of blood, hanging over butcher shops,
only the flash of a knife, only violence.

from the cycle Castle

4

Journey on, merchants and monks,
      squires and knights,
journey on, motley masses of craftsmen,
      along the Vilnia and the Neris.
Unblock the frothing sun
      rolling through the half-blank city
and drink from your hands –
      this stone city turns eternal here.
Greeted in so many tongues,
      place a round stone each…
Here the wind blows from rivers through alleys.
      Steaming
with harsh motley sounds, dawn breaks.
      Don't fear going blind –
Babylon will not rise in this world,
      but stone-walled Vilnius instead.
Don't tear your stunned eyes from
      morning's light white clouds,
reflected in the confluence,
      becoming belfries.
Silversmiths, salt-sellers and cobblers,
      may you live here in concord.
All homeless wanderers of goodwill –
      may you build this Vilnius.

Girl with Ermine

In the pastry shop, under reproductions –
     Botticelli and Leonardo da Vinci –
a dark-haired girl in jeans
     hides ermine softness in her heart.
Beyond closed doors –
     childhood flies through Old Town
        on a borrowed bike.

– I will know you by your strange eyes,
     or your caress-smoothed hair…

Cinnamon, vanilla and sun.
     Shining walls of Sunday silence.
A dark-haired girl in jeans
     drinks coffee, scattering dusty tunes.
Beyond closed doors –
     a springtime street,
        and souls – are spanned.

– I will know you by your black beads,
     or the trembling of your fingers…

Air Raid

Pompeo Girolamo Batoni's 'The Penitent Magdalene', bombed by British-American forces while in a wagon of paintings on a Dresden street, February, 1945. From the history of paintings...

Mary Magdalene,
    fair-haired, gentle sinner,
Mary Magdalene,
    wearing classicism's mantle of unearthly blue,
Mary Magdalene,
    with an open, dusty book of prayer
    resting on a skull at night,
Mary Magdalene,
    painted with oils in a sunny master's studio,
Mary Magdalene,
    half-naked among sputtering candle flames,
Mary Magdalene,
    fondled by monks, thieves and Roman electors,
Mary Magdalene,
    letting down your long-gone hair like the rays of the sun,
Mary Magdalene,
    from the bomb-shelter –
    that bottomless cellar of brotherhood,
Mary Magdalene,
    from the drunken haunts of blood-stained soldiers,
Mary Magdalene,
    a starving recluse
    in 20th century libraries,
Mary Magdalene,
    tortured in the ghetto, the gestapo HQ
    or in a concentration camp,
Mary Magdalene,
    losing your form – becoming soul,
Mary Magdalene,
    redeeming sins beneath airplane wings,
Mary Magdalene,

on a burnt-out Dresden street,
forgive us,
hear us,
have mercy on us...

Store

Again the marble counter is covered
    with blood and sunlight.
Again it is slaughtering-day in the old town store.
    Again the butcher smiles,
having wiped the blood off his hands.
    Again Handel plays on the radio.
Again the branching dog rose blooms
    above the black-haired buyer.

Coronation

Cover my shivering shoulders
with November's leaves
like a mantle of mink.
In that capital, for me –
only dead-end streets.
     Touch
the crown beneath the kerchief
of my humbled head.
Don't divine a basket
in my hands, but a sceptre.
     Don't cut through
the sidewalk boards – it's a bridge.
I'm here – under ashberry pearls.

But a curse – like an honorary title –
falls from the drunken king of clubs.

Crystal

When my palms pine for your skin
     and you aren't there,
every night, my hope is stretched and honed.
This many-sided, clear light
     is crystal's law
because longing grows like diamonds and salt.
Even in the darkest vein of insomnia,
     silence shimmers
with a strange harmony
     remaining out of reach –
untouchable and unweighed –
     a precious stone
sparkling on an October street
     through mud and bluster…

A Nameless Source

Like a nameless source below the cathedral,
like a spray of light within a pall of fog,
open yourself, and come to life once more.
Water your heart with no remorse.

Try to be like the sky – cold and blue –
or gaze at the gulls above the Neris as if
through an arrow-slit in the castle wall,
but only when their wings are full of wind for you.

Groan like the brash ice, or hiss like the slush
that melts in the flow of the street –
for this is the voice, returning to the sun,
the one you took from a nameless source.

To Gather Geraniums Yet

To gather geraniums yet
for the hallway's windowsill,
to darn again black tights
while yellow petals unfurl –

like a masterpiece without a fake,
clarified by morning's ray –
to smile still through the ache
in front of the mirror's grey,

each day deeper yet – to January,
into the jaws of solitude's flat,
to carry the profile secretly,
like the germ of life, by the heart.

Vilnius. Archaeology

We dug up brick walls,
      the opening of a door or gate,
a platform of cold stone –
      the sky always sinking below –
we dug up the rumble of a road,
      the exposed rock of a sombre past.

We dug up a miserable Troy,
      an impoverished, little Pompeii,
the city's sunken, sacred horizons
      – limestone grown ulcerous,
we dug up our roots from stone
      – we found them full of pain.

We dug up again the limpid edge
      of a dream, an ice abyss,
a tall quarry of crystal –
      the heart still beating on the left,
we dug up the verdure of tiles,
      and the flame of a candle which
we shelter in our hands from the wind.

Siauroji Street

Where a courtyard like a shell
      guards a small, graceful church,
where green shutters twine, and a window
      opens onto smutty snow,
onto a cross-section of pavement,
      onto the lives of clay,
      onto the depths below peat
where the tree's god has rotted away,
      where the sun's magical wheel
still guards the fireplace's flame,
      the bronze patina sand,
the thousand-year-old skull of a bear,
      a boar's tooth amulet,
then a ghostly, bewitching leap above it
      into medieval clay
where the street turns deeper
      towards the undiscovered ford of the Neris.

The Defensive Wall of the City

Vines wind round an arrow-slit
    and the cinema doors,
but the gates still creak in an airless space,
    perhaps still opening in a dream –
perhaps a guard still stands in the niche against the Tartar horde –
    I nudge the gate open
onto twilight and garlands of ivy
    that sway above Vilnius engraved:
the defensive ruins, and a nameless spring,
    or just the cold flow of the Styx –
I walk along the nonexistent wall
    that twists and turns through my subconscious,
but the gates and towers only lie in the album of Vilnius' sights,
    in the silence of old watercolours
by Smuglewicz –
    a hopeful and vital maple tree spreads
among bricks and crumbling blocks
    that fended off fire and blood and pitch –
cemented, they still hold up my home,
    and get under my skin like the greatest works of old.

By Steamboat

The slow, dark-green river water
  will be this summer's mirror,
dragonflies and butterflies play in the sun,
  two scrawny seagulls,
a drake, glossy in the reeds –
  the moment in which you understand
the enchantment of sailing through summer's garden,
  the glittering
reflections of the shore, shadows of bridges,
  that whole August landscape
of river and harbour, the shoal by the castle,
  the shocking strength
of feeling, the blue lane of acacias –
  upon embarking from the steamboat,
wonder's joy – damp pebbles
  like pearls in your hand,
yellow wildflowers blooming late,
  marsh marigolds
and buttercups swimming in the stream,
  sunflowers sway in the wind,
shocks of rye in a field at twilight,
  rose hips
by the trolley bus stop
  beginning to clarify your blood.

Anapaestic

1.

Let me hear again the insomniac lark that sings
from the scent of lilacs blossoming blue, through foggy nights
when the balcony over the town becomes a stage
like the endless horizon of dawn – please don't take from me
this sleepless world where the pale and intricate stars
still fill the heart with light in a sacred hour of solitude
when the waking city enlarges the sky in a violet haze,
or when water murmurs under the bridges in ice-free streams.

2.

Ancient calendars with layouts of Vilnius's historic streets,
ancient calendars with brazen clocks of the dead marking time,
the ivies a century old, the courtyard's arch wound in thin
spiderweb speech, blocking you off from home,
where on my table a pile of faded notes grows,
all used and forgotten beside the telephones that no longer hear,
and the empty address books – I'm afraid of your murmur,
for the bloody past is turned into strophes under skies
bound up with fog, their memory fills – until one bitter day
amber leaves will fall on caryatids dozing away.

3.

Let the seasons change like chrysanthemums in a vase,
now turning brown, as their soft undulations appear in a barber shop mirror,
and the face which you left in the dark as the trolley bus groaned
its meandering tread through the starless and soulless night of November's
       sterility –
with your hair in the barber shop mirror again, let your sadness fall with it too,
forget once more how a hopeless anxiety hounds us day after day,
and embrace the chrysanthemum's charming weave, why wait?
The pedestrians, streets, and cities still swarm –
these are the visions in the mirror of twilight's barber shop.

4.

It's the thaw's living water – just celesta, celesta, celesta I hear,
with the light that drips into my brain from the snowy window,
it's forbidden to be silent here like a marble mask on the wall,
we're allowed to sing naturally, in a joy without struggle, pure –
I can see the unfolding blossoms of begonias on fire in a vase
on a sill, made of clay, with the scent of the earth, in the middle of the day –
but the sun of the thaw still sparkles cold and pale over the city,
in the balcony doors, the rays of the sun are like ivy winding around.

Clear Night

A boy's choir – from the rustle of yellowing leaves,
yes, it must be – with purple cassocks and white collars,
gloria – caressing my hair, you swim into moonlight,
an image on the retina, comprehended without sight.

Violets on the wet ground, shepherd's purse, meadow-grass,
yes, it's the indescribable, unsinkable autumn, like ambergris.
The city shines silver in a mist, limitless and deeply asleep.
Night grows clear in your room that almost glows green.

Yes, a clarifying power seeps through our wonder,
and everything depends on a glance, a ray, I remember
all of it as in a dream, touching – the walls parting –
and the silver, inlaid with jade, an Aztec stone, a ring.

Fuchsia Branch in the Wind

I block the sea's wind from the branch.
My black umbrella shelters it from rain.
Its blossom's flames put me in a trance.
I fear a reckless touch might bring them pain.

The sea howls as with a coming hurricane.
Clouds grow leaden, dim. The sky leers –
and the fragile fuchsia flutters in vain.
A black flag is raised upon the pier.

The branch in my hand lives in colour.
Its delicate petals lean from lightning,
hide from thunder – the passion, the horror.
September so rarely storms. What frightens

me is the flash that flares the flower distinct
in the window of the night – for just one blink
of an eye – my only September bloom…
The sea storms so much it shakes the room.

The Street Ship

At the crossroads, the bow points into dusk.
Lights flicker in tight, airless rooms. The foundation
shivers as darkness pummels the gunwales,
eaten by rust. (Multi-coloured dreams spread
from its arching alcoves like Viking sails
braided by the yard's flora, inflated by wind.)
You stood here once – a pulsing red ember,
throbbing in midsummer rain. Now, the crumbling facade
drifts into darkness, coming apart, sails chafed
by the sun's remains. The ship is stuck in shallows,
and the castaway seeds of a few happy nights
stick to my palm. Fruit trees rustle and flow.

Concert

Vivaldi and the breeze, the breeze, the breeze,
it's only the breeze of the evening growing rosy,

only the darkening park, before the fall of dew,
and the symphony playing on a terrace by the blue

sea, only clouds, streaming to the eerie light,
it's only five flapping ducks in wild flight,

only gulls and swallows swiftly leaving ardent
marks of shade like lacquer on the rose garden,

and the bird calls fall on the largo that fades away,
leaving only murmuring waves, only candles in bay

windows, blossoms crumbling, and summer closed
by pain, by only, and already, the scent of wilting roses.

Amber Gems

Amber gems polished by shifting sands,
rough, old amulets shining in the sun –
for a woman short of happiness – storm-loved,
limpid gems like a morning wave, eyes
I will not see, thrust into the gloaming,
        driven by gyres –
amber gems washed in the spume of the sea –
fires on the hill, stakes,
        lighthouses by drifts
of time's moving sand,
        gems of my ancestors:
rivets of boats, stoney net plummets,
ashes in the fireplace,
        baskets of flounder
buried in damp sand –
        above prongs of fog: ribbons
of constellations from the bronze age,
        above the auroras of boats,
boggy, overgrown pools –
        a place of sacrifice in the dunes,
a raspberry bloated with blood
        of Teutonic Knights and local Kurs.

Blue Earth

To dig each day in the blue earth –
     to mine amber
while the sea moans through dunes…
       Once again, you find in your dreams
an ingot of resinous gold
       containing a primitive plant phantasm.
You dig every night in the sombre ruins of Crete and Troy
     searching for
the old sun, the fragment of a ray,
     what time hasn't wiped away –
encased in fog, pictures of the past
     where the amber lacquer
of Alexandria shines
     on ancient Roman instruments –
every day, every night, preserving
      this sacred treasure –
to dig into blue earth,
     into darkness, between clods,
to find that shard of happiness, that one drop,
     that clearest piece of amber
which your ancestors placed in the grave
     at dawn, engraving with flint
the head of a moose
     so that you would meet no ill fate,
so that your endless horizons
     would be free of clouds –
this is your sea, your sky,
     your blue earth.

Ladybug

The sun's wing,
       sleeping on winter's foggy sill –
be warmed by my scent –
       millennial life
flutters on your pinions, eternal and vital –
when you recover on my palm, happiness comes.
You have landed like a drop of blood,
       like a fire's spark
on a cluttered writing desk,
       on an old diary
where one forgotten want still quivers –
fly high into the deep and distant pagan sky.

Seven-spotted week – seven days of sun –
like a card in my hand, pulled from fate's deck.

Old Town (I)

The green between cracked sidewalk stones –
the barely sprouted bent grass, the hoary plantain –
and on the roofs, on banisters of balconies,
wandering seeds are taking root –
the stinging stamen of thistle,
the swaying purple willow herb,
the blind heddle, the green…
O the green rays of life
in a wasteland of stone!
The blue stars of widow flower and chicory
flicker through the cracks of brick walls
in secluded courtyards and garages –
red buds of geraniums light
the sombre window of a dilapidated house –
in drought, in heat, through thunderstorm,
the lion's jaws roar between windowsills,
the wing of a plaster cupid flutters,
grass spurts from out of the steps,
the street is a wilderness –
the broken echo of poetry,
the savage, intoxicating victory of life…
The bleak heat of garbage dumps,
the neglect of forgotten dead-end streets,
endless –
old fireplaces shattered
by wormwood, burdock and nettles.

Sunflower

In Vilnius, in a construction site on Tartar Street,
    a sunflower grew last year –
a flower of green, alien blood,
    always turned to the sun,
last summer's symbol –
    I still hear its murmur in the wind,
I still see its golden ring of leaves,
    dusty and bright,
a flower of green, alien blood,
    as if sprouting from the Vilnius baroque,
it rocked its noble head up high
    above the sleepy heat of scattered
bricks, above debris,
    above foundations previously unseen,
    above the medieval town
with my royal summer park,
    on top of breaking glass – O wind,
play another madrigal above the iron stubble,
    an echo is audible from last year
in this waste land of heat, last summer's penurious
    flower changing its golden face again
to gaze through clouds of dust.

Vytis

The heraldic horseman flies –
      a white-armoured horseman,
a gravestone horseman,
      the horseman of the official seal –
      I feel the wind of Žalgiris
blowing into my eyes –
      still warm after hundreds of years,
I feel the flame of my fatherland's fire,
      mournful and bitter –
the cloth of flags –
      the blood of Žalgiris,
      the blood of gulags,
bending in the breeze –
      the shining knight flies above Vilnius
and his horse's shoes spark,
      and his shining sword
glitters in the sun,
      his shield bears a cross –
      the silver warrior
fighting for freedom,
      the horseman honouring
the hopes of our ancestors,
      Traidenis, Algirdas and Vytautas,
their ancient heraldic sign.

Bend

I still see the horse-bridge and old city gates
like ghosts by Saint Katherine's Church,
the tile roofs, stone arches, a few windy
arrow slits, the water under pavement
that is cool and pure – ages flow
in the sunken river under streets,
campaniles and chapels – springs
are reborn in its sombre stream,
and in my solitude
I still hear, from the balcony, the purling
of water under buildings – at the crossroads
it bends into another branch, and its spray
under the earth is light that splashes my dream.

Like Two Beasts of Babylon

Two broken, concrete lions guard
the door of a dilapidated, two-story house,
like two beasts of Babylon,
under white acacia blooms.
Cold rain,
sadness like fog,
a dripping branch
casts a threatening shadow,
and you stop for a second,
having closed the bookstore doors –
a strange world awaits,
secret and glowing, in the book
you carry home in your hands
to a house, shabby and dismal,
a street running north by the river,
yet a cold spring rain stirs in your veins –
faster, faster, fiercely –
two beasts of Babylon,
two broken, concrete lions lie.

Moonflowers

Selena's plants – the moon's flowers,
all kinds of white flowers, especially those
whose scent is stronger in darkness –
the bouquet of lilies through the new moon,
angel's trumpets along a fence, campion
shining for planets, galaxies, stars,
a field of narcotic white poppies,
wild plums in moonlight, or the first anemones
through a drift of snow, maybe the quivering bells
of lilies of the valley, perhaps a bird-cherry branch
over water,
             or maybe milfoil,
or a blanching jasmine tree, or cotton grass
in a swamp, with pollen soft as lamb's wool in mist –
Selena's pastured silver herd,
or childhood's white clover wreath
dropped on pavement,
a lily blossom above the water's depths,
vegetation from the bottom of the sea of dreams,
Selena's plants – the moon's flowers.

Lilacs on Pylimo Street

Lilacs, cut down by the Vilnius synagogue,
still shine with clusters of violet light,
still fragrant, dusted with gasoline, the heavy
lilacs, cut down by the Vilnius synagogue,
still echo a rusted bell from the railroad –
the dead city's undying soul –
lilacs, cut down by the Vilnius synagogue,
still shine with clusters of violet light.

from the cycle Sunday in Old Town

5.

The gladiator's flower –
        a blood-spattered gladiolus.
I see it in the gloaming
        when the sword of a ray
rips its hue from darkness –
        the half-empty frame of a marketplace
floods with the radiance of embers…

        Feel my lips
like a wet caress
        on its blade –
        for there was
no battle…
        Darker by the heartbeat,
        it has a beauty
that isn't ours.
        In the arena – in the square,
        it's so quiet that it rings,
and the unawaited emptiness cuts to the brain.

Drought (II)

Mad city heat
with wide-open windows
on heavy, fetid, sweltering twilights –
when above the dusty trees,
above the parking
lots, bats
fly
dumb with humidity –
this dismal summer
with the stench of cemeteries,
when my dead sister's golden mirror
retains my impressed reflection
like a twin,
when a fire burns in the street by the parched fountain –
the tenement roof flames into the night,
when the comet's pearl necklace
pierces Jupiter's face –
a time of crumbling icebergs,
when my nerves drink in
this midsummer cosmic catastrophe
with its twinkling cold fragments in the sky,
and throughout the drought
I echo within my knocking heart.

from the cycle Vilnius Churches

3. Saint Katherine's, or Benedictine's Church

Their hands stretched to embrace –
      or maybe to bless:
      angels, apostles, saints –
hands from the pleats of statues fluttering in the draft,
      from rose shadows and azure
      through dirty gold,
through dust, filth and rust –
      apostles, saints, bishops,
      hands for us sinners, stretched
in dark humidity,
      when clouds sink low,
      when the storm gathers,
      when rain closes out the rays,
a baroque theatre –
      Sibyl and Anne, noblemen's daughters, nuns
      who march from the nunnery
      through the ruined church
on the gallery floor covered
      with the Pacas family's fleurs-de-lis –
      ashen marble splits
and smoky frescos chafe – disgraced,
      their cherry colours,
      their blue-greens, grown over with mold –
they march with candles in the first procession
      to a still soft chanting in the church,
      having left it to the barbarians.

A Grey, Northern House

A black dove, here, like the soul of Semiramis,
flown, perhaps, from the towers of Babylon –
a storm may blow us some blossoms and seeds,
and a warm scent, come from some clay waste,
will make me feel the roots' connection to the leaves –
and with double cedar doors opening in a dream,
it may seem once more that someone
touches my cheek through ancient varnish
and silently sheds tears.
A grey, northern house emerges on my street
where three winged lions perch on a pediment,
where autumns of solitude reign like austere sunsets,
where bodiless time runs like the Euphrates,
driven by wind, filled with boats –
the majestic motions of a woman,
a lapis-lazuli necklace shining in moonlight,
a howl from the statues' jaws in the night...

Street Light

At night – lights of the boulevard,
  moonlight
  in a darkened room,
burning lamps, advertisements shine
  even in this starless,
  severe midnight –
street light comes with the cry
  of a hounded animal
  driven into a corner –
it comes with evening bells,
  with the stench of gateways,
  with smoke in the mouth,
at night – light from the heart of darkness,
  from its depths,
  from the capital's jungles,
street light
  through nightlife
  deathly oppressive in its cheer.

Street Performer

He could be a street performer
    with a white cat
    curled over his shoulder –
a measly coin
    occasionally dribbles
    into his holey hat,
and he, carefree, could be on stage
    in the sunlit city –
    the solitary beggar
who wandered in from somewhere
    to a place of angry faces,
    still manages a smile –
his grey locks,
    his lively, black eyes:
    a street performer,
the last before the new millennium,
    like a soul,
    or seen from up close –
a shadow of Italianate Vilnius –
    picturesquely sentimental
    between Old Town walls,
his cat like snow,
    lazy and white –
    clouds swim by, dreary and dull.

A Bell from the Vilnius Fair

Warmed by my hands:
      a small earthenware bell
      from the town-hall fair –
what an amazing sound
      beneath the high, autumn sky
      still filled with sun,
I hear an echo
      of Vilnius's ancient bells,
      and it fills me with cheer.
The voice of those who lived here –
      let it ring
      through the fog,
let this heart of clay,
      resonant from fire,
      wind blowing dust and ashes away,
echo –
      a little, earthenware bell
      from the Vilnius Old Town fair.

I Saw a Snowy Madonna

I saw a snow Madonna
     on the evening of Three Kings –
she was standing barefoot on a cloud
     in an old picture frame
     in St. Raphael's Church in Vilnius
on the bank of the river at dusk,
     where statues of foreign soldiers stand at the bridge,
     where winter rules the dilapidated scene,
     where only the snow comes in waves,
and where in the one lit window there flamed
     maybe a candle, maybe a star.

Under Electra's Virginal Statue

Under Electra's virginal statue
    above the city sunk into gloom,
the river freezes, blended with night,
    between December's banks –
winter stings the street,
    even smiles go out – yet, continually patient,
with flurries above the frozen river's crook,
    you plumb the depths
under Electra's light
    where the Neris runs by the hospital pane –
it's already winter – you grasp at life now
    like a pulsing vein.

Wagon

The railroad tracks will emerge
    from last century's red brick
      station, overgrown with ivy.
The train window will frame a solitary birch,
      then marshes, ravines…
     And in the narrow, swaying wagon,
checking tickets, once again, the conductor
    will stop in front of you,
     and you will be short a few measly cents
for happiness,
     and you will stand alone, pushing the walls
     with your palms, already tracked by the years…
Still, while the bolt hasn't yet struck,
     you will travel on with your standing ticket
     and feel a wild, divine weight, a charge –
left with the poor,
     you will yearn for a ray of light
     like the spark of childhood, hot and true.

Glossary

Algirdas: see *Traidenis* below.

Barboras: A reference to Barbora Radvilaitė (see under *Radvilaitė* below).

Bona (Queen): Bona Sforza (1494-1557), of the House of Sforza, rulers of Milan, married King Sigismund I the Old, becoming Queen of Poland, heavily involved in affairs of state, mother of Sigismund II Augustus.

Cabiria: The main character in Federico Fellini's film *Nights of Cabiria*, a prostitute whose attempts at romantic fulfillment lead to her being robbed, jilted, pushed into a river, and almost pushed off a cliff.

Catherine of the Habsburgs: Catherine of Austria (1533-1572), member of the House of Habsburg, third wife of Sigismund II Augustus, Queen of Poland, sister of Elisabeth (see below).

Curonian: Of or relating to the area of the Curonians or Kurs, a Baltic people who inhabited what is now western Latvia and Lithuania until their merger with modern Latvians and Lithuanians. The sandy peninsula in the Baltic Sea, named after them the Curonian Spit, extends from the Kaliningrad enclave of Russia to Lithuania.

Elisabeth of the Habsburgs: Elizabeth of Austria (1526-1545), member of the House of Habsburg, first wife of Sigismund II Augustus (see below); she died within a year of their marriage.

Goštautas: Stanislovas Goštautas (1507-1542) of the noble Goštautai family in the Grand Duchy of Lithuania, married Barbora Radvilaitė in 1537; their marriage was childless.

Moniuszko: Stanisław Moniuszko, a Polish composer of the 19th century, a founding figure in Polish opera.

Kurs: Curonians (see above).

Mikolojus Radvila "the Red": Mikołaj Radziwiłł (1512-1584), brother of Barbora Radvilaitė, cousin to Mikolojus Radvila "the Black" (see below), opposed to political union with Poland.

Mikolojus Radvila "the Black": Mikołaj Radziwiłł (1515-1565) cousin to Barbora Radvilaitė and her brother Mikolojus Radvila "the Red", opposed to political union with Poland.

Livonian: Of or relating to the Finnic peoples of northern Latvia and southern

Estonia. The Livonian language (of the Uralic family) is now considered extinct.

Neris: One of Lithuania's two major rivers. From its source in Belarus it flows through Vilnius and into the Nemunas at Kaunas.

Prussian: Of or relating to the Baltic region that is now occupied, more or less, by the Kaliningrad enclave of Russia. The Prussian people were of the Baltic family and were finally conquered and assimilated under the occupation of the German Teutonic Knights, starting from the 13th century.

Pylimo Street: "Embankment Street", forming one border of the Old Town of Vilnius, running just outside the former wall of the old city.

Barbora Radvilaitė: Barbara Radziwiłł (1520/23-1551), the daughter of the noble Radziwiłł family (*Radvilai* in Lithuanian) of Vilnius, a great beauty who became the mistress of King Sigismund II Augustus of Poland and Lithuania. They were married in secret against his mother's (Bona Sforza's) wishes (as well as the opposition of the Polish nobility), and she died of illness (some say poisoning) a year later.

Siauroji Street: "Narrow Street", in the Old Town of Vilnius.

Sigismund / Sigismund Augustus: Sigismund II Augustus (1520-1572), King of Poland and Lithuania, last of the Jagiellon dynasty (that began with the Lithuanian Grand Duke Jogaila, see below under Traidenis).

Smuglewicz: Franciszek Smuglewicz (1745-1807), a Polish-Lithuanian painter and engraver of historical and architectural themes, including many famous scenes of old Vilnius.

Teutonic Knights: A German monastic military order founded in Acre, Kingdom of Jerusalem, 1190, to carry out the crusades in the Near East, then transferred to what was Baltic Prussia in order to pursue a campaign of converting the pagan Baltic peoples to Christianity by force, an endeavor that was effected by means of military conquest and occupation.

Traidenis, *Algirdas* and *Vytautas*: Three Grand Dukes of Lithuania. Traidenis ruled from 1270 to his death in 1282. Algirdas (1296-1377) was the father of Jogaila, later king of Poland (as Władysław II Jagiełło). Vytautas (1350-1430) was Algirdas' nephew, Jogaila's cousin, and became known as Vytautas the Great for his expansion of the Grand Duchy of Lithuanian from the Baltic to Black seas.

Ula: Ula Vaičiūnaitė, daughter of Judita Vaičiūnaitė.

Vilnia: Or, *Vilnelė*, a small river that flows from its source in Belarus into the Neris next to the medieval castle of Vilnius.

Vytis: The coat of arms of Lithuania consisting of a mounted knight brandishing a sword and bearing a shield emblazoned with a double cross.

Žalgiris: A battle, also known as *Grunwald* and *Tannenberg*, in 1410 in which a combined force of Lithuanians and Poles – with assistance from some Czechs and Tatars – under the battlefield leadership of Grand Duke Vytautas (q.v.), and the overall command of Jogaila (Władysław II Jagiełło), King of Poland and Lithuania, defeated the Teutonic Knights (q.v.), dealing them a crushing blow from which they never fully recovered.